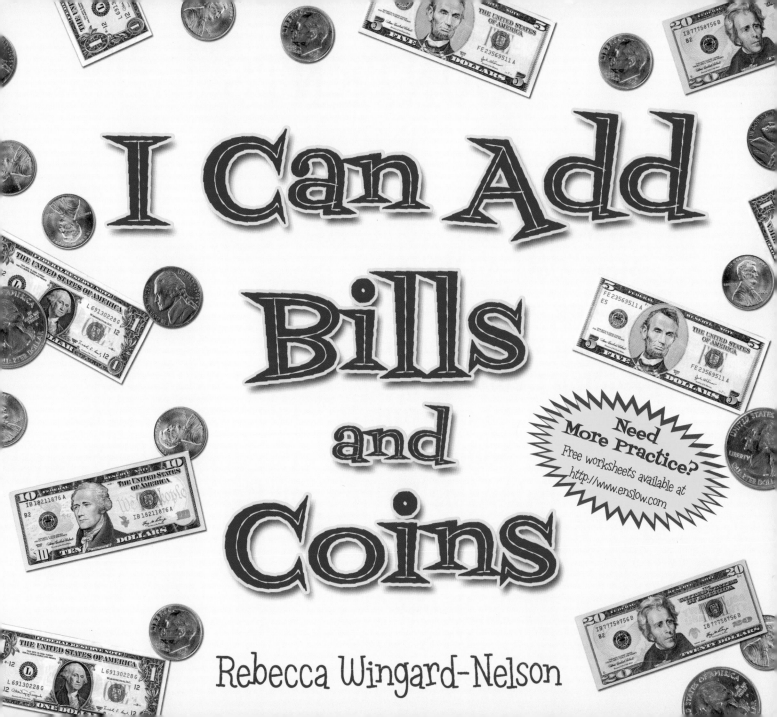

I Can Add Bills and Coins

Rebecca Wingard-Nelson

CONTENTS

Coins and Bills

 penny
1¢

 one-dollar bill
$1

 nickel
5¢

 five-dollar bill
$5

 dime
10¢

 ten-dollar bill
$10

 quarter
25¢

 twenty-dollar
bill
$20

Coins Plus More Coins

You have 2 nickels and 6 pennies.

How much money do you have in all?

There are two different ways to find the answer.

One way is to put the coins together and count their value. Start with the first coin, then "count on."

5¢   10¢   11¢   12¢   13¢   14¢   15¢   16¢

Another way is to add the value of the nickels and the value of the pennies.

Coins	Value	
2 nickels	10¢	10¢
6 pennies	6¢	+ 6¢
		16¢

Either way, you get 16¢ in all.

So Many Coins

12 nickels + 22 pennies

How much money in all?

When you have many coins, you can find the value of each *kind* of coin first. Then add.

What is the value of the nickels?
Count by 5s to find the value of 12 nickels.

5¢ 10¢ 15¢ 20¢ 25¢ 30¢
35¢ 40¢ 45¢ 50¢ 55¢ 60¢

The value of the nickels is 60¢.

What is the value of the pennies?
Each penny has a value of
1¢, so 22 pennies have a
value of 22¢.

Add the value of the nickels and the value of the pennies.

Coins	Value	
12 nickels	60¢	60¢
22 pennies	22¢	+ 22¢
		82¢

There is 82¢ in all.

More Coin Addition

1 dime + 3 nickels + 14 pennies

How much money in all?

You can count on to find the value of the coins.

10¢   15¢   20¢   25¢

26¢   27¢   28¢   29¢   30¢   31¢   32¢

33¢   34¢   35¢   36¢   37¢   38¢   39¢

Or you can add the values of the dime, nickels, and pennies.

Coins	Value
1 dime	10¢
3 nickels	15¢
14 pennies	14¢

$$\begin{array}{r} 10¢ \\ 15¢ \\ + \quad 14¢ \\ \hline 9 \end{array}$$

First, add the digits in the ones place.
$0 + 5 + 4 = 9$

$$\begin{array}{r} 10¢ \\ 15¢ \\ + \quad 14¢ \\ \hline 39¢ \end{array}$$

Then add the digits in the tens place.
$1 + 1 + 1 = 3$

Either way, you get 39¢ in all.

Adding Sets of Coins

**You have 1 dime and 3 pennies in your hand.
You have 1 nickel and 3 pennies in your pocket.
How much money do you have in all?**

The coins in your hand
are 1 dime and 3 pennies.
You have 13¢.

10¢   11¢   12¢   13¢

The coins in your pocket
are 1 nickel and 3 pennies.
You have 8¢.

5¢   6¢   7¢   8¢

You can put the coins together and count the value.

10¢ 15¢ 16¢ 17¢ 18¢ 19¢ 20¢ 21¢

Or you can add the value of the coins in your pocket to the value of the coins in your hand.

	Value	
hand	13¢	13¢
pocket	8¢	+ 8¢
		21¢

Either way, you have 21¢ in all.

Adding With Quarters

You have 2 quarters and 4 pennies.
You find 1 quarter, 1 dime, and 2 nickels.
How much money do you have in all?

2 quarters and
4 pennies are 54¢.

25¢

50¢

51¢

52¢

53¢

54¢

1 quarter, 1 dime, and
2 nickels are 45¢.

25¢

35¢

40¢

45¢

You can put the coins together and count the value.

25¢
50¢
75¢
85¢
90¢
95¢
96¢
97¢
98¢
99¢

Or you can add the value of the coins you have and the value of the coins you find.

	Value	
have	54¢	54¢
find	45¢	+ 45¢
		99¢

Either way, you have 99¢ in all.

Adding Cents

You have 65¢ in one hand. You have 25¢ in the other hand. How much do you have in both hands?

Do you need to know what kind of coins are in each hand? NO! You know the value of the coins in each hand.

Add the value in one hand to the value in the other hand.

$$
\begin{array}{r}
{}^{1} \\
65¢ \\
+\ 25¢ \\
\hline
90¢
\end{array}
$$

**You had 82¢. You found another 41¢.
How much money do you have now?**

Add the money you started with, 82¢,
and the money you found, 41¢.

$$\begin{array}{r} 82¢ \\ +\ 41¢ \\ \hline 123¢ \end{array}$$

You now have 123¢.

When an amount of money is
100¢ or more, it is written using
a dollar sign and a decimal point.
100¢ = $1.00, or one dollar.

dollar sign → **$1.**23 ← decimal point

dollars   cents

123¢ = $1.23
$1.23 is read "one dollar and twenty-three cents."

You have $1.23 in all.

Adding Bills

You have 3 ten-dollar bills and 11 one-dollar bills. How many dollars do you have in all?

One way to find how much money you have in all is to put the bills together and count the value of them.

$10 $20 $30

$31 $32 $33 $34 $35 $36 $37 $38 $39 $40 $41

Or you can add the value of the ten-dollar bills and the value of the one-dollar bills.

Bills	Value	
3 ten-dollar bills	$30	$30
11 one-dollar bills	$11	+ $11
		$41

Either way, you have $41 in all.

Adding Dollars

You have $36 in your wallet. You have $43 in your pocket. How many dollars do you have in all?

Do you need to know what kind of bills you have? NO! You know the value of the dollars in your wallet, and the value of the dollars in your pocket.

Add the dollars in your wallet and the dollars in your pocket.

$$\begin{array}{r} \$36 \\ + \ \$43 \\ \hline \$79 \end{array}$$

You have $16. Your mother gives you 2 five-dollar bills. How much money do you have in all?

Do you need to know what kind of bills you started with? NO!

What is the value of
2 five-dollar bills?
Count by 5s to find the value.

$5

$10

Add the dollars you had to the dollars your mother gave you.

dollars you had + dollars your mother
                          gave you

$16   + $10   = $26

You have $26 in all.

Adding Dollars and Cents

What is the value of 1 five-dollar bill and 1 quarter?

Write the values of the bill and coin using dollar signs and decimal points.

$5.00

Coins or Bills	Value
1 five-dollar bill	$5.00
1 quarter	$0.25

$0.25

Write the value of the bill and coin together.

$5.25

dollars   cents

$5.25 is read "five dollars and twenty-five cents."

You have $10.25. You earn another $5.50. How much money do you have in all?

Add money values like whole numbers.

Line up the decimal points.
First add the cents.

$10.25
+ $ 5.50
.75

Then add the dollars.

$10.25
+ $ 5.50
$15.75

You have $15.75 in all.

LET'S REVIEW

Find the value of a group of coins by counting on OR adding.

Find the value of a group of bills by counting on OR adding.

You can add money amounts without knowing the names of the coins or bills.

Money values can be written in three different ways:

SYMBOL	EXAMPLE	WHEN TO USE
cent symbol	50¢	for amounts less than one dollar
dollar symbol	$13	for even dollar amounts
dollar symbol and decimal point	$16.75	for any money value

LEARN MORE

Books

Cooper, Jason. *American Coins and Bills*. Vero Beach, Fla.:
  Rourke Publishing, 2003.

Hill, Mary. *Dollars*. New York: Children's Press, 2005.

Roverson, Erin. *All About Money*. New York: Children's
  Press, 2004.

Web Sites

H.I.P. Pocket Change
  <http://www.usmint.gov/kids/>

U.S. Treasury–For Kids
  <http://www.ustreas.gov/kids/>

INDEX

Enslow Elementary, an imprint of Enslow Publishers, Inc.

Enslow Elementary® is a registered trademark of Enslow Publishers, Inc.

Copyright © 2010 by Enslow Publishers, Inc.

All rights reserved.

No part of this book may be reproduced by any means without the written permission of the publisher.

Library of Congress Cataloging-in-Publication Data

Wingard-Nelson, Rebecca.
    I can add bills and coins / Rebecca Wingard-Nelson
        p. cm. — (I like money math!)
        Summary: "An introduction to adding money for young readers"—Provided by publisher.
        Includes bibliographical references and index.
        ISBN: 978-0-7660-3143-2
        1. Addition—Juvenile literature. 2. Money—United States—Juvenile literature.
I. Title.
        QA115.W7534 2010
        513.2'11—dc22   2009006488

ISBN-13: 978-0-7660-3657-4 (paperback)
ISBN-10: 0-7660-3657-X (paperback)

Printed in the United States of America
012012 Lake Book Manufacturing, Inc., Melrose Park, IL
10 9 8 7 6 5 4 3 2 1

To Our Readers: We have done our best to make sure all Internet Addresses in this book were active and appropriate when we went to press. However, the author and the publisher have no control over and assume no liability for the material available on those Internet sites or on other Web sites they may link to. Any comments or suggestions can be sent by e-mail to comments@enslow.com or to the address on the back cover.

♻ Enslow Publishers, Inc., is committed to printing our books on recycled paper. The paper in every book contains 10% to 30% post-consumer waste (PCW). The cover board on the outside of each book contains 100% PCW. Our goal is to do our part to help young people and the environment too!

Photo Credits: Shutterstock

Cover Photo: Shutterstock

Enslow Elementary
an imprint of
Enslow Publishers, Inc.
40 Industrial Road
Box 398
Berkeley Heights, NJ 07922
USA
http://www.enslow.com